ADVENTURES IN COLD PLACES

PACKED FULL OF ACTIVITIES AND OVER 250 STICKERS

A little baby polar bear is hiding in this book! Look for him on every main sticker scene.

THE ARCTIC

NORTH POLE

ALASKA

THE SWISS ALPS

MONTREAL

THE SAHARA DESER

THE ANDES

There's a flag for
each place you'll be exploring.
Find the matching stickers
at the end of your book
and stick them in the
right places.

COLD WORLD

Wow! This picture shows all of the countries in the world. It shows all the cold places in your book.

ICE HOTEL

MOSCOW

HARBIN

Count how many ships and animals there are bobbing in the water. Can you spot an orca, a blue whale and a narwhal?

SOUTH POLE

ANTARCTICA

READY TO GO!

Make an adventure pass to explore cold places!
First write your details, then add your stamp stickers.

My Adventure Pass

Name

Age

Stick your stamp here.

Draw your face here.

Cold Places Postcard

Draw what you did today on the postcard.
Then write the name of someone to send it to.

Don't forget to create a stamp!

NORTH POLE

THE ARCTIC

Brrrrr, sail to the frrrrreezing Arctic with us and explore the floating icebergs where polar bears live with their friends.

Did you know that an orca can grow to be 23 feet (7 metres) long? That's like four grown-ups lying head to toe.

Fill the sledge with things for the Arctic. We need a warm coat, gloves and goggles!

Have fun filling the icebergs with animals lounging, swimming, playing and diving.

Polar bears have pads on their feet. The rough surface is like sandpaper to stop them slipping on the ice.

Give this fluffy harp seal some pups.

Can you spot a tail poking out of the water? It's a narwhal, the unicorn of the sea! Give him some friends with your stickers.

Can you see an Arctic skua stealing a fish? Some people call them avian pirates because they like to take other animals' food.

THE ARCTIC
is full of snowy white animals who live on the ice. These special creatures have clever ways of surviving the freezing temperatures.

Hold on tight

Our white fur helps us to camouflage!

I'm the biggest hunter on land!

COSY POLAR BEARS

Can you give the polar bears bright scarves and hats?

Find the fish and paint them blue.

How many baby polar bears are sleeping?

SWITZERLAND

This is a Swiss Franc

We're going to have lots of fun sledging, waving at snowboarders, learning to ski and drinking hot chocolate.

Fill the wooden log box with things for the Swiss Alps. Don't forget a woolly hat, snow boots and some fluffy ear muffs!

Grüezi

Whoosh!
Look! The children are learning to ski. Add some more with your stickers.
Add more people sledging down the hill and playing in the snow.
Moo!
Yummy hot chocolate
Add your stickers to the picture to make it look brilliant!

People come to Wengen in the **SWISS ALPS** to ski, toboggan and play in the snow. There are no cars in the village so people travel by train or on a cable car instead.

The people want to hear music. Stick on somebody playing an alphorn.

Can you spot a person singing a special song? This is called yodeling!

MOUNTAIN GOATS

Give the goats red and blue hats.

Make the goats' bells yellow.

Can you spot the naughty goat eating his hat?

Buenos días

Come and explore
the Andes mountains in Peru,
South America. We can't wait
to wave at llamas, see amazing
stripy mountains and meet
beautiful dolls made of wool.

This is a Nuevo
sol coin

PERU

Tomatoes and
potatoes are used the
world over, but they
were first found in
the Andes mountains!

Add your stickers
to the Peruvian
cushion! Look for a
cheeky little guinea
pig and some yummy
food from Peru.

13

Use your stickers to add people and animals to the amazing mountains.

Look for a herd of nibbling guinea pigs and add some more.

Hum

Alpacas tell you how they feel by humming, snorting, clucking, grumbling, screeching or screaming.

14

THE ANDES

In faraway Ausangate, Peru, the mountains are so high they can make some people feel sick. You have to be very fit and healthy to visit this beautiful land.

Wow! Can you spot a huge flying condor? Add another in the sky.

This woman is making special clothes using alpaca wool.

Squeak Squeak Squeak!

15

PERUVIAN DOLLS

Make their costumes nice and bright!

Can you spot the alpaca? make him yellow.

Can you find the rosy cheeks and make them red?

16

We're travelling to Alaska, USA! We're really excited about zooming in a plane that can land on water and having a feast outside where bears might come and take our food!

Here is a US dollar.

USA

Totem poles can be short or tall. They are ofen used to tell stories by the people who make them.

Hi

Help us pack a picnic to take with us on our adventure! Find your stickers and add them to the picnic basket.

Floatplanes fly and then land on water. Add a floatplane in the sky and one on the river.
Have you seen my family?
Trumpeter swans make a loud tooting sound like a trumpet. Add some more to the picture.
Add lots of people and bears to the picture with your stickers!

The Taku River in **ALASKA** is well known for its floatplanes that land on the water. The people here are stopping off for lunch and some big furry friends want to share their meal!

Quick! This man wants to take a photo of the bears. Can you give him his camera?

Toooot!

Can you spot the hungry bears waiting by the grill? Give them some tasty salmon to eat.

Grrrr!

TOTEM POLES

Make the totem poles nice and bright!

Can you find the eagle's head? Give him a bright yellow beak.

Can you spot two rabbits? Give them pink noses.

Can you find the fish and make it red?

Bonjour

CANADA

We're going to Montreal, Canada. Come and have fun snow-sliding in the park, spotting beavers and building brilliant snow people!

Here is a Canadian dollar.

The Biosphere is a museum in Montreal shaped like a snow globe, where you can learn all about the environment!

The beaver stores all sorts of things in his lodge. Put your sporty stickers in his lodge too!

This acrobat is from the Cirque du Soleil, a famous circus from Montreal that travels all over the world!

The Mount Royal Park in **MONTREAL** is lots of fun in winter. There are all kinds of activities for families to enjoy together.

Ice hockey is a very popular sport in Canada. If you find ice too slippery, you can always try field hockey.

Here's a beaver. Give him a friend. He has big sharp teeth and a long flat tail!

iCE SKATiNG

Make the skaters' costumes eye-catching!

Can you spot the ice hockey player? Give him a red suit.

How many skating beavers can you spot?

Find the skater with the flowery skirt and give her red hair.

SWEDEN

Hej!

Let's have fun exploring Swedish Lapland. We can't wait to stay up late, ride on a sledge pulled by reindeer and see magical lights swirling in the sky!

This is a 5 krona coin

Pack everything you need into the skidoo! Don't forget your skis, poles and snow shoes! I think a husky wants to come too!

This building in Malmo looks like a twisted body. It's called the Turning Torso.

25

Add lots of people enjoying the night sky from the Ice Hotel.
When the Northern Lights appear, they make the night sky look purple, green, pink and yellow! Wow!
Wahoo!
Give these huskies a friend to help them pull the sled.

THE iCE HOTEL
is made completely out of ice! People stay here then go on night-time adventures to hunt for the Northern Lights.

MOOSE CROSSING

This man is using a chainsaw to carve a beautiful ice sculpture. Give him some food to keep him warm.

BARKING HUSKIES

Make their collars green, blue and red!

Find the huskies' bones and make them yellow.

Make sure their collars are bright so they stand out in the snow.

Privet

We're travelling to Siberia, Russia. Let's meet reindeer and see amazing animals that live in a freezing underwater world.

This is a ruble note.

RUSSiA

Most people know this beautiful building as St Basil's Cathedral, but its full name is the Cathedral of the Protection of Most Holy Theotokos on the Moat.

Dress the diver ready for the cold Siberian waters of Lake Baikal. She needs her snorkel, belt and goggles.

Neigh! neigh!
Sometimes Lake Baikal is completely frozen on the surface. The ice is so thick that a train once chugged over it.
Baikal seals can stay underwater for a really long time! Add some more swimming deep in the lake.
Have fun adding creatures and divers to the picture.
Hi, I'm an amphipod!

This man is chipping ice from the lake so he can make tea. Find a sticker to give him a nice cup of hot tea now.

I'd love a cup of tea.

LAKE BAIKAL

in Russia is the oldest and deepest lake in the world. Lots of creatures in the lake are endemic. That means you can't see them anywhere else on the planet.

The largest flatworm on earth lives here. See if you can spot him and give him a twin. He looks like a flat, squashed worm!

ROAMING REINDEER
Make these reindeer bright and beautiful.

Find the reindeer wearing rugs on their backs, and make them bright.

Find the bells and paint them yellow.

How many baby reindeer can you see?

32

Come and visit a snow and ice festival in Harbin, China, with us. We can't wait to see giant snowmen, huge fireworks and play on a slide made from ice!

This is a 20 yuán note.

CHINA

This poor man is very cold. Give him some warm trousers, gloves, a woolly hat and a hot drink in a flask to warm him up!

Ni hao!

Did you know that they use the ice from the lake to make the ice hotel and carve these beautiful sculptures? It then melts and they start all over again the next year.

Add people having fun at the festival and fill the sky with fireworks.

BANG! It's firework time. Light up the sky with your stickers.

Cheese! Look for a snow bear with a camera and give him a snow hat.

Put on some people whizzing down this slide made from ice.

HARBIN

in China has some of the biggest and best snowmen in the world. Every night the city is lit up so the snow and ice shines every shade of the rainbow.

Which ice sculpture do you like best? Add some people looking up at it.

YUMMY FOOD

Bring the dishes to life with your bright pencils!

Which bowls have little flowers? Turn the flowers yellow.

Look for all the bowls with chopsticks in and make them green.

Count how many faces you can see on the bowls?

MOROCCO

Come and explore the Sahara Desert, Morocco, with us! We'll be riding camels, meeting desert hedgehogs and snuggling in tents to keep us warm at night.

This is a Dirham coin.

Salaam

Fill the Moroccan carpet bag with stickers. You'll need a warm blanket and a water bottle, and don't forget your torch!

A group of camels is called a caravan! Find your stickers and make a caravan of camels.

Fennec foxes are tiny but they have extremely big ears! Add some to the desert.

Find your stickers and fill the night-time desert with people and animals.

People in Morocco like to drink hot sweet mint tea. Give the people a nice hot drink to enjoy.

People travel to Erg Chebbi in the **SAHARA DESERT** to camp next to giant hills made from sand. The Sahara is the largest hot desert in the world, but at night time it can be freezing!

These people need a tent! Can you put one up for them?

I like to come out at night because it's nice and cool.

Can I have some tea please?

DUNG BEETLES!

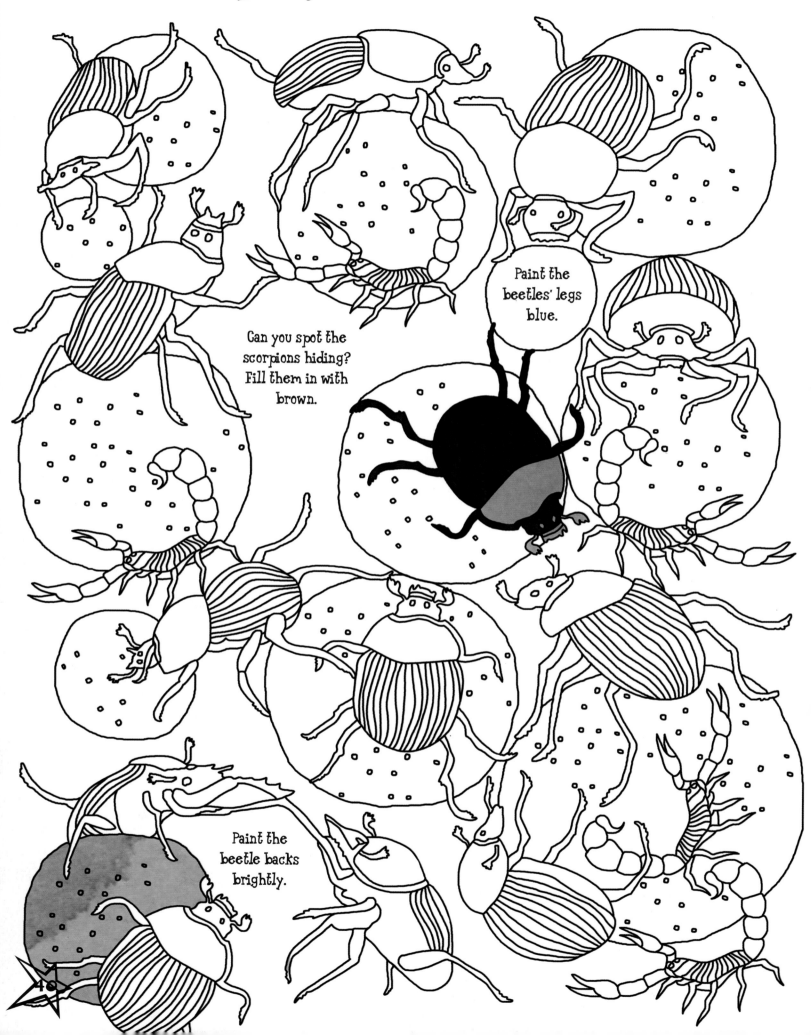

Paint the beetles' legs blue.

Can you spot the scorpions hiding? Fill them in with brown.

Paint the beetle backs brightly.

Come along on our adventure to find penguins in Antarctica. We'll look out for giant whales and meet the people who work on this land made of ice.

Hi

ANTARCTICA

SOUTH POLE

WOW! Emperor penguins have four layers of feathers to protect them from the icy winds. It also gives them a waterproof coat!

Fill the fishing bag with creatures from the icy waters.

Did you know that Antarctica is the coldest place on earth?

Add tourists, people working and plenty of penguins to icy Antarctica.

Stick on some Emperor penguins huddling together. How do you keep warm on a cold day?

I blow bubbles to help me catch fish!

Huddling keeps us warm and cosy.

Wave at the waddling Adelie penguins and then try waddling around the room!

ANTARCTICA

is big, cold, windy and dry so nobody lives here all of the time. People do work and visit, but there are a lot more penguins than people!

Add some people zooming in a skidoo, a special vehicle that can drive on ice.

WADDLING PENGUINS Have fun decorating these waddling friends!

How many sealions can you spot?

Can you spot the baby penguins with gloves on? Make them nice and bright!

ANTARCTICA DIFFERENCES

Spot 6 differences between these two pictures.

Answers on page 48

COLD SHADOWS

Can you match the busy creatures with their shadows?
Draw a line with your crayon from the picture to its shadow.

Answers on page 48

MOViNG MAZE

Pick your ride and see where the road will take you.

Answers on page 48

ANSWERS FOR PAGES 45, 46 AND 47

ANTARCTICA DIFFERENCES

BUSY SHADOWS

MOVING MAZE

1. The fish changes to pink in picture 2
2. The little penguin's scarf, at the front, disappears in picture 2
3. The fish tucked under the penguin's flipper disappears in picture 2
4. One of the big penguins at the back disappears in picture 2
5. One of the baby penguins disappears in picture 2
6. The little penguin peeping from behind the iceberg disappears in picture 2

1. The helicopter takes you to the cow
2. The huskies take you to the twisted tower
3. The boat takes you to the research centre
4. The seaplane takes you to the barbecue

Published in October 2014 by Lonely Planet Publications Pty Ltd
ABN 36 005 607 983
www.lonelyplanet.com
ISBN 978 1 74360 395 6
© Lonely Planet 2014
© Photographs as indicated 2014
Printed in China   10 9 8 7 6 5 4 3 2

Publishing Director	Piers Pickard
Publisher	Mina Patria
Art Director & Designer	Beverley Speight
Author	Sara Oldham
Illustrator	Kremina Dimitrova
Pre-press production	Tag Response
Print production	Larissa Frost
Thanks to	Jessica Cole, Dan Tucker

Photo credits

Lonely Planet offices

AUSTRALIA
90 Maribyrnong St, Footscray, Victoria, 3011, Australia
Phone 03 8379 8000 **Email talk2us@lonelyplanet.com.au**

USA
150 Linden St, Oakland, CA 94607
Phone 510 250 6400 **Email info@lonelyplanet.com**

UNITED KINGDOM
Media Centre, 201 Wood Lane, London W12 7TQ
Phone 020 8433 1333 **Email go@lonelyplanet.co.uk**

Montreal
p.22-23

The Ice Hotel
p.26-27

Sahara
p.38-39

Antarctica p.42-43

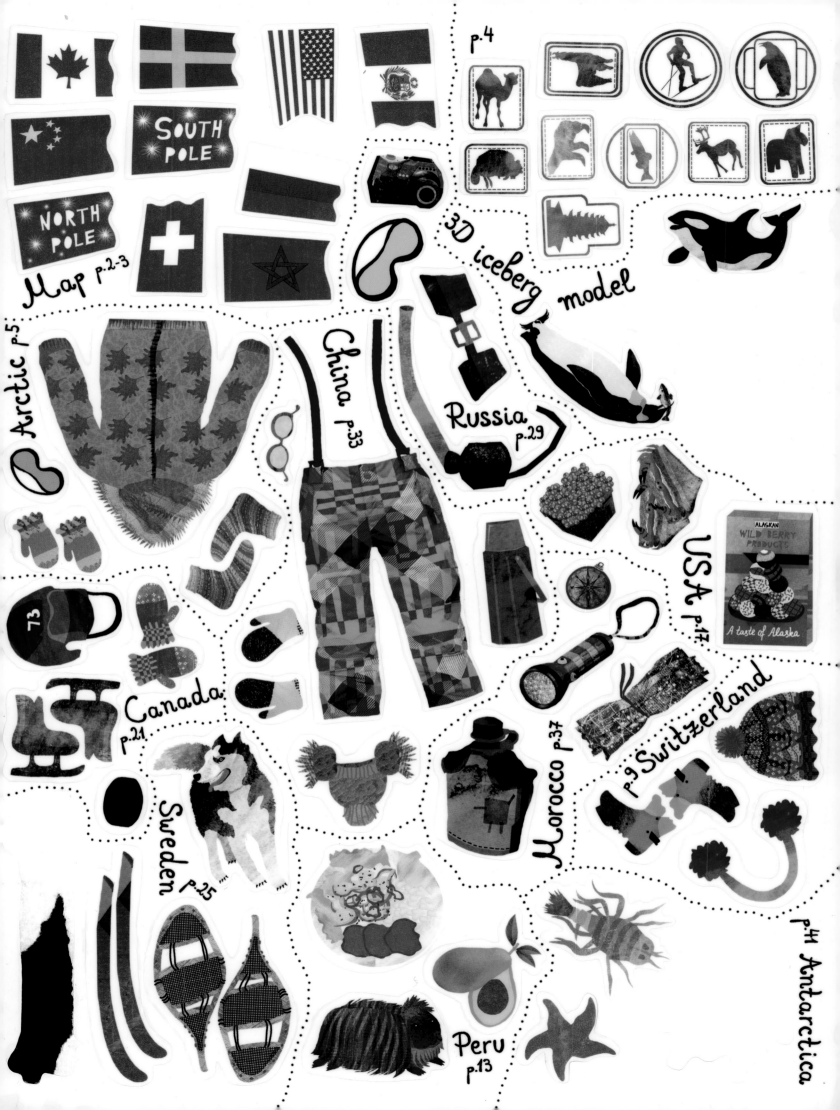